HAYNES EXPLAINS
PETS

Owners' Workshop Manual

© Haynes Publishing • Written by **Boris Starling**

Published in September 2017

A catalogue record for this book is available from the British Library

ISBN 978 1 78521 153 9

Haynes Publishing, Sparkford, Yeovil, Somerset BA22 7JJ, UK
Tel: +44 (0) 1963 440635
Website: www.haynes.com

Haynes North America, Inc.,
861 Lawrence Drive, Newbury Park, California 91320, USA

Printed and bound in Malaysia

Cover image from Getty Images

Illustrations taken from the Haynes Austin/MG Metro Owners Workshop Manual

Safety first!

Pets can be dangerous. Don't let their veneer of domestication fool you, not for a second. Dogs can bite. Snakes can try to poison or suffocate you. Rodents often carry disease. And cats – let's not even get started on the need for caution around cats. See the way the cat is looking at you through narrowed eyes? That look should make you very scared. Being around cats is like being at the poker table: there's always a sucker there, and if you can't see who it is then it's you.

Working facilities

Optimum working facilities vary according to the pet. Cats don't really care whether they have 10 square metres or 10 square miles, because in their heads they're bossing the whole damn world anyway. As for dogs, whatever the limit is for them to come to heel when you call them, their optimum is A Little Bit Beyond. Hamsters and goldfish just go round and round and round and round. Snakes are happy with a branch on which to chill.

Contents

Introduction

The British are a nation of pet lovers. More than half the population have at least one pet, and there are almost as many pets (58m) as there are people (65m). Britain was the first nation to found an animal welfare charity, and stories of animal cruelty cause more outrage than almost any other subject. Nine out of 10 pet owners consider their pets as members of their family. Two-thirds of Britons believe their pets are more reliable than their partners (something which will probably not surprise readers of *Haynes Explains Marriage*) and one-third buy presents for their pets more often than they do for their partner. The two things might not be unconnected, come to think of it. Maybe those people who want to marry their pets aren't as mad as we all thought they were.

About this manual

The aim of this manual is to help you get the best value from your pets. It can do this in several ways. It can help you (a) decide what work must be done (b) tackle this work yourself, though you may choose to have much of it performed by external contractors such as the professional dog walker, who has biceps the size of Arnie's from the need to hold onto the leads of a dozen different mutts at once, or the old dear down the road to whom your tabby cat has taken quite the shine despite all that you do for her, the ungrateful so-and-so (the cat, that is, not the old dear).

The manual has drawings and descriptions to show the function and layout of the various components. Tasks are described in a logical order so that even a novice can do the work. Although the specific requirements of a pet vary according to species, fundamentally they all want the same thing: food, water, shelter, and the inestimable satisfaction of waking you up at 3am by demanding to be let in/let out/fed/heard. They can then go back to sleep for the next 18 hours with a smug pet smile on their smug pet face, the little sods.

Dimensions, weights and capacities

Overall height

Cats .... 9–10in (23–25cm). Rises to 14in with fur standing
.... on end and 648in at apogee of startled jump.
Dogs............................. 4in (Chihuahua) – 44in (Great Dane). 44in! Those
.... (very) high hurdles in the Olympics are only 36in!
Snakes .... we ain't about height, baby. We about length. See below.

Overall length

Cats .... 18in (46cm) head and body, 12in (30cm) tail.
Dogs............................. 4in (10cm) – 98in (250cm). One was a Yorkshire Terrier,
.... the other an English mastiff. No prizes for guessing
.... which was which.
Snakes .... 4in (10cm) – 25ft (8m). If you have an 8m python
.... at home then you need either a medal or sectioning.

Consumption

Cats .... Fish. Mice. Assorted small animals they kill and bring to
.... you like a posh restaurant where they show you the food
.... before cooking it.
Dogs............................. Meat. Anything they or another dog has regurgitated.
.... Anything they or another dog has… you get the picture.
.... And millions of pieces of homework, obviously.
Snakes .... Rodents. Birds. Frogs. And according to urban legend,
.... if a python straightens itself out, it's measuring you up.

Engine

Stroke............................. yes please, especially for cats and dogs.
Power .... all to our feline overlords, naturally.
Torque .... 638Nm from twisting motion of dog chasing own tail.
Bore............................. Nothing personal, but the goldfish doesn't exactly have
.... a sparkling conversational repertoire.

MODEL LINE: FELINE
Lifespan

As any fule kno, a cat has nine lives rather than the bluff old traditionalist one which we humans have to be satisfied with (Glenn Hoddle, if you're reading this, let's not go there again with the reincarnation and karma stuff). As the old proverb goes: 'a cat has nine lives. For three he plays, for three he strays, and for the last three he stays.' Sounds like a few politicians I can think of.

The whole 'nine lives' malarkey has several serious implications for the feline model. For a start, insurance policies are ruinously expensive, as are lawyers' fees for the nine separate wills which need to be drawn up. Knowing cats' propensity for endlessly going in and out of a house (see Behaviour), the 'nine lives' thing may well have stemmed from the first cat ever to die and arrive at the Pearly Gates, where it stalked in and out, in and out until St Peter got bored and turfed it back down to earth.

Curiosity killed the cat – presumably not until eight lives had already passed

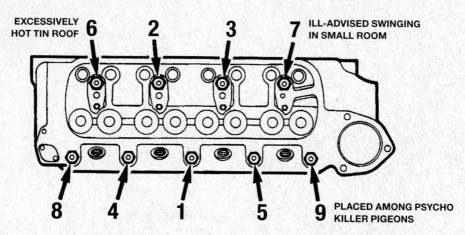

EXCESSIVELY HOT TIN ROOF **6**   **2**   **3**   **7** ILL-ADVISED SWINGING IN SMALL ROOM

8   **4**   **1**   **5**   **9** PLACED AMONG PSYCHO KILLER PIGEONS

FIG 6•1 **THREE TIMES THREE: PROGRAMMING MULTIPLE FELINE EXISTENCES**

⚠ Self-righting system

Cats are extremely good at righting themselves in mid-air, offering excellent rollover protection. Feline body mechanics dictate that a cat in freefall rotates its head to face upwards, arches its back (it has 30 vertebrae compared to a human's 24, making it much more supple than any person other than the ones you see in those 'yoga' videos and spreads its legs beneath to take the weight as it lands.

A cat actually bends in the middle so that the front half of its body rotates about a different axis from the rear half. A falling cat is therefore less like an aeroplane and more like a parachute – its terminal velocity is half that of a human's.

There is of course a subsection of the 'falling cat' issue, which is the 'falling buttered cat' effect. If a cat always lands on its feet, and a piece of buttered toast always lands buttered side down (or almost always: in a University study, 81 of 100 buttered toast slices dropped from a table under laboratory conditions landed buttered side down DO SOME REAL WORK YOU BLOODY STUDENTS), then a cat with a piece of buttered toast strapped to its back will simply rotate endlessly a short distance above the ground as the two opposing forces (cat-twisting and butter repulsion) cancel each other out. The potential implications of this for the transport industry are twofold.

1. Perpetual energy
The cat simply spins endlessly without losing speed. A sufficient number of toast-laden felines placed at strategic intervals could power a hyperloop monorail system and thus revolutionise land-based high-speed travel.

2. Anti-gravity
Since the cat/toast construct can fall from a given point but cannot land, by definition it defies gravity and can therefore be repurposed as a BFAD (Buttered Feline Antigravity Drive). (A prototype of dairy-based antigravity methods was demonstrated with unverified reports of cows jumping over the moon.) When the aliens do finally arrive, they will almost certainly have travelled at lightspeed using these very BFADs. Which would make all the cats currently on earth sort of sleeper agents for the invasion, like the pods in *War Of The Worlds*. It's all making sense now.

Note: *experiment does not work if you use (a) margarine (b) I Can't Believe It's Not Butter (c) brandy butter (d) Harry Potter butterbeer (e) butterflies.*

Model behaviour

The feline model exhibits many distinct patterns of behaviour.

a) Follows human to bathroom. Stares at human while human goes to loo. Stares at human while human takes shower. Stares at human while human takes bath. Stares at human while human shaves, cleans teeth, applies moisturiser, etc. If human remonstrates, continues to stare. If human shuts door in face, continues to stare so human gets freaked out when human eventually emerges.

MODULE 101
– CONTRARINESS

MODULE 102
– SASSINESS

FIG 6•2 FELINE BEHAVIOUR
MODULES, PART ONE

b) When made to look uncool – e.g. falls off chair while cleaning self, gets stuck in box – always gives an 'I totally meant to do that' look. Never shows weakness. Pulls out a little 'whatevs' and a lot of sass. Never laughs at self. Is always the straight guy. Retains coolness and superiority at all costs. If human laughs, flicks them the tail and walks away with strut like Travolta at the end of *Saturday Night Fever*.

c) When offered a variety of surfaces and locations on which to lie, always chooses (a) the most uncomfortable (b) the one which will inconvenience the human the most. A £100 cat bed in the corner of the room is no good. Half on the floor and half on human's knees is optimal.

d) Kills small animal. Mutilates small animal. Brings small animal into house for human's edification. Puts small animal on human's favourite cushion or pillow. When human shouts 'HOW MANY TIMES HAVE I TOLD YOU NOT TO BRING A MOUSE/RAT/BIRD/VOLE INTO THE HOUSE?' resists temptation to smile.

e) Stands inside back door loudly demanding to go out. Goes out. Stands outside back door loudly demanding to come in. Comes in. Repeats. Repeats. Repeats. Especially on a door which has a perfectly good catflap.

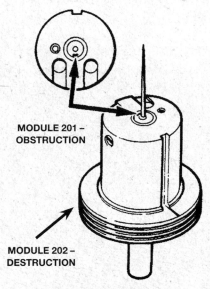

MODULE 201 –
OBSTRUCTION

MODULE 202 –
DESTRUCTION

FIG 6•3 **FELINE BEHAVIOUR
MODULES, PART TWO**

f) Observes human watching electronic flickery picture box thing. Calculates distance between human and box, orientation of human to box, and sector of viewing angle as result of those two factors. Positions self between human and box at optimum distance and orientation to obscure as much of flickering box from human as possible.

g) Does not get into human's bed except (a) when human trying to change the sheets and duvet cover (b) when human needs to wake up at 4am because cat decides that human needs too.

h) Every day, does something to remind human of truth of adage 'you can have a cat or you can have plants, but you cannot have both.' When last plant is finally removed from house, performs dance as though scorer of winning touchdown in SuperBowl. Knows full well what SuperBowl is as has prevented human from watching it.

i) Sees toilet roll. Claws at toilet roll until end comes loose. Pulls toilet roll out to full extent until bathroom looks like inside of an ancient Egyptian tomb (ancient Egypt being of course the acme of civilisation as the people there treated cats like gods). Considers work done.

j) Gives human withering look now and then. Just because.

k) Coughs up hairballs. Leaves them on floor. Knows human will pick them up.

l) Observes human working on laptop. Climbs onto human's lap. Observes what human is working on. Considers pointing out typographical errors (Word documents) or numerical ones (Excel spreadsheets) to human. Decides against it.

m) Looks at clock. Sees it says 3pm Runs up and down stairs at high speed repeatedly until 4pm Every day. Knows that human doesn't understand why, so also knows that human will never understand that the reason why feline does this is because feline knows that human will never understand.

n) Rolls on back to demand that human rubs tummy. Refuses to reciprocate when human lying on back. Human must be reminded that this relationship is strictly one-way.

o) Sees something on a surface. Checks to see whether permanently attached or just resting there. If latter, nudges it until it reaches edge of surface and falls off. Delighted to see that object doesn't right itself in mid-air and is therefore obviously not feline. Especially effective when (a) object is breakable (b) floor is hard.

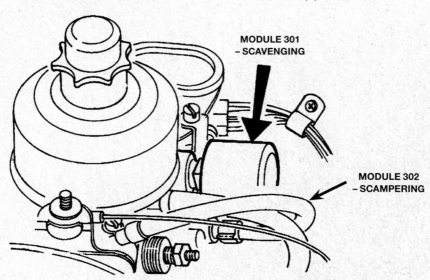

MODULE 301
– SCAVENGING

MODULE 302
– SCAMPERING

FIG 6•4 **FELINE BEHAVIOUR MODULES, PART THREE**

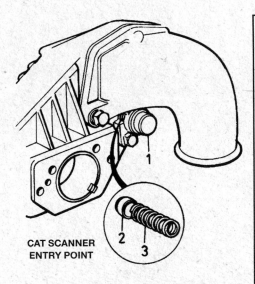

CAT SCANNER ENTRY POINT

FIG 6•5 **FELINE PERSONALITY ASSESSING MACHINE**

Cat culture

In ancient Egypt, the people would write on walls and worship cats. Three millennia later, they still do. Nowadays it's called the Internet. The Internet is the greatest revolution in mass communication since Johannes Guttenberg invented printed books (see *Haynes Explains Germans*). Guttenberg concentrated on the dominant cultural force of the time, religion, and made Bibles. The Internet does the same for cats. Every cat video you laugh at, every feline meme you 'like' or share, is just another step on the long road towards the Cataclysm, the feline takeover of the world. (There is a slim possibility that they may get beaten to this by a bovine takeover if cows ever learn to cross cattle grids. This will be called the Apocowlypse.)

In summary

Cats dislike everything that doesn't directly contribute to their own comfort, hate change, treat the rest of the world with contempt and expect to be waited on hand and foot.

Researchers in Edinburgh and the Bronx found that domestic house cats have very similar personalities to African lions. Both groups have high inclinations toward dominance, impulsiveness and neuroticism. Basically, if your cat was bigger it would kill you.

Receives present from human. Stupid present. Nice box, though. Ignores present. Plays with box. Gets in box. Very nice box.

Women drivers

The phrase 'Cat Lady' comes with several word associations attached: unmarried, unfashionable and unhinged. Scientists and lexicographers alike are divided as to the precise definition of Cat Lady. How many cats does one need to be a Cat Lady? How old does one have to be to qualify? These are the important questions our government should be wrestling with rather than all that Brexit hoo-hah (though doubtless somewhere in the EU's trillion pages of regulations there are indeed recommendations from a pan-European working group as to what exactly constitutes a Cat Lady).

Luckily Haynes Explains is on hand with a short Twenty Questions quiz so you can tell whether or not you're in danger of becoming a Cat Lady. Gentlemen, you need not take this quiz. There are plenty aimed at you in *Haynes Explains Football*.

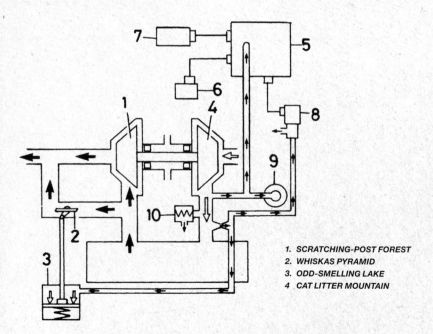

1. SCRATCHING-POST FOREST
2. WHISKAS PYRAMID
3. ODD-SMELLING LAKE
4. CAT LITTER MOUNTAIN

FIG 6•6 **CAT LADY'S DOMESTIC ACCOMMODATION: A SCHEMATIC**

So you think you're a Cat Lady

1) Do you sit outside the local Tesco with a tinfoil hat on ranting at passers-by about CIA mind control and shapeshifting lizards?

2) Do you ask your cats what they think of any dates you have?

3) Do you ask your cats what they think of your friends?

4) Do you come home from work and tell your cats all about your day?

5) Can you only sleep if at least one cat is in bed with you?

6) Do you alter your sleeping position to accommodate your cat?

7) Do you see the relationship between yourself and your cats as akin to that between Snow White and her dwarves, Ali Baba and his thieves or Gladys Knight and her Pips?

8) Do you spend more on food for your cats than you do on food for yourself?

9) Do you spend more on lint rollers than on toilet paper?

10) Do you spend more on Christmas presents for the cats in your life than you do for the humans in your life?

11) Do you own cat-themed items of clothing?

12) Do you spend more time grooming your cats than you do yourself?

13) Have you stopped wearing certain coloured clothing because the amount of cat hairs which contrast against it make you look like Chewbacca/a polar bear/a gorilla (delete as appropriate)?

14) Do you save boxes from delivery packages for your cats to play in?

15) Do you delay going up to bed or to the bathroom if a cat is sitting on your lap?

16) When you do finally move, do you apologise profusely to the cat in question?

17) Do one or more of your cats feature in your social media profile pictures?

18) Do one or more of your cats have a social media account of their own?

19) Do you clean the cat litter boxes first thing every morning? As in, literally before coffee and breakfast?

20) Do you put spells on those who have crossed you?

Score

0	You're fine
1-5	Cat Lady Lite
6-10	Regular Cat Lady
11-15	Serious Cat Lady
16-20	Hardcore Cat Lady

Famous models

The Cheshire Cat
Sits in a tree and often fades away until only his smile is left. Never explained precisely what he has to be so happy about, the smug git.

The Cat In The Hat
Speaks mainly in rhymes, which pitches him halfway between Wordsworth and Eminem. Not to be confused with either the cat sitting on the mat or The Twat In The Hat.

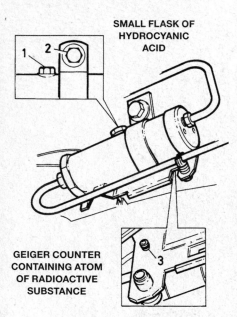

SMALL FLASK OF HYDROCYANIC ACID

GEIGER COUNTER CONTAINING ATOM OF RADIOACTIVE SUBSTANCE

FIG 6•7 **STEEL CHAMBER HOME OF SCHRÖDINGER'S CAT**

Garfield
Fat orange cat who is a self-satisfied narcissistic sadist. Any comparisons with current world leaders is presumably unintentional but rather prescient given that he was 'born' in 1978. Also realistic in that he regards both humans (Jon) and dogs (Odie) with amused contempt.

Schrödinger's Cat
Subject of a philosophical conundrum which sees said cat in a locked steel chamber with his existence depending on the state of a radioactive atom, and therefore both technically alive and dead until the box is opened and its actual state revealed (presumably including 'rather pissed off' if it's still alive). Not to be confused with

a) its Wild West outlaw cousin who was Wanted Dead & Alive
b) its Japanese cousin Hello Kitty Goodbye Kitty
c) its alcoholic joke cousin who walks into a bar and doesn't
d) Schrödinger's Immigrant, simultaneously too lazy to work but also coming over here and stealing all our jobs.

⚠ Feline dictionary

Word	Definition
Catacomb	What a cat has next to its hairbrush.
Catalogue	Glossy booklet for cats to peruse the latest in feline fashion.
Catarrh	Feline pirate.
Catcall	When the phone rings and you hand it to your moggy with the words 'it's for you'.
Caterpillar	Method of propulsion for feline tanks.
Catfish	A fish who is happy he's not a dogfish but pretty pissed off about everything else.
Cathedral	Where cats go to be worshipped.
Catholic	A cat who drinks too much.
Catnap	18 hours a day if you're feline. 18 minutes a day if you're human, waking up with a jolt and dribble on your chin when the train arrives at Slade Green.
Catwalk	In human terms, where the Beautiful People strut their stuff. For cats, an everyday promenade. Cat Deeley.

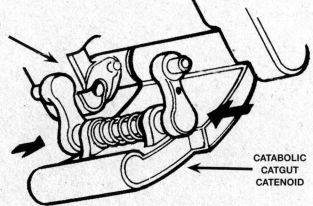

CATENATED
CATOPTRIC
CATHODE

CATABOLIC
CATGUT
CATENOID

FIG 6•8 **CATAMENIAL CATHETERISING CATALYSER**

MODEL LINE: CANINE
Model behaviour

Whereas cats sincerely believe they are rulers of the world and masters of the universe, dogs know that humans are in charge. That's why they're man's best friend, because unlike wives, children and cats they actually listen to us men and give us back some small measure of self-esteem which we desperately need in these over-emasculating times. Dogs: cheaper than therapy.

Dogs have been domesticated for tens of thousands of years, and in that time deliberately bred by humans to suit our needs, whether those needs be working dogs, protection dogs, ornamental dogs or hot dogs. (Maybe *Haynes Explains Americans* might be a better place for the last one). Cats, as established earlier, are basically small lions and more sociopathic than Hannibal Lecter.

Cats have retractable claws and dogs don't. Cats therefore keep their claws sharp where dogs blunt theirs through constant wear. This makes sense on so many levels.

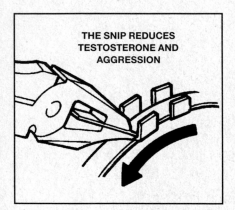

THE SNIP REDUCES
TESTOSTERONE AND
AGGRESSION

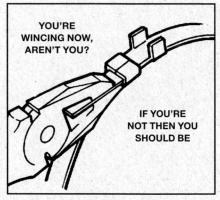

YOU'RE
WINCING NOW,
AREN'T YOU?

IF YOU'RE
NOT THEN YOU
SHOULD BE

FIG 6•9 **CANINE BEHAVIOUR MODULE: NEUTERING**

Patterns of behaviour

The canine model exhibits many distinct patterns of behaviour.

a) Not very good at 'knock knock' jokes, as goes mental every time hears a knock at the door.

....

b) Not very good at being in an orchestra either, as spends all the time waiting for the conductor to throw that darn stick he's waving around.

....

c) Very good at head tilt to soften human's heart whenever human says 'no'. Has optimum angle and soulful eyes look down pat.

....

d) Gets very, very excited when going out of the door. Gets very, very excited when coming back in through door. What did I miss? What I did miss? Anything happen when I was gone?

....

e) Loves swimming in lakes or rivers. Loves goofing around with hosepipes in summer. Hates bathtime. Go figure.

....

f) Has several beds dotted around the house. Prefers the humans' bed. Knows human always vowed before having dog not to let dog sleep on bed. Sees human clinging on to the 20% of bed area left. Smirks.

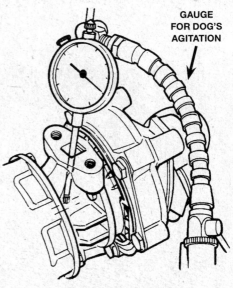

GAUGE FOR DOG'S AGITATION

FIG 6•10 **CANINE BEHAVIOUR MODULE: HOOVER DISCOMFORT**

g) Greet human like long-lost brother when human returns from short trip to shops. Jump around, follow human everywhere, wag tail and lick human. Human remembers he forgot the milk. Human goes back to shops. Human returns from shops again. Enthusiastic greetings repeated.

....

h) Knows exactly the one day of the year when human walker has forgotten the poop bag, and celebrates this day by doing enormous turd in the middle of the busiest street available.

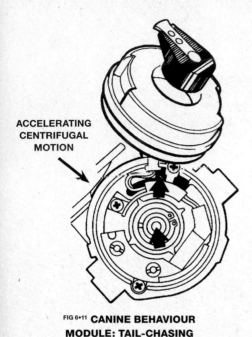

**ACCELERATING
CENTRIFUGAL
MOTION**

FIG 6•11 **CANINE BEHAVIOUR
MODULE: TAIL-CHASING**

i) Loves licking human's face
especially immediately after
(a) self-grooming in unsavoury area
(b) drinking water from toilet bowl.

j) When accused of anything –
stealing food, turfing sofa cushions
onto floor, making mess – goes
with patented Shaggy Defence:
'It Wasn't Me.' (NB: 'Shaggy'
refers in this instance to the
singer Orville Richard Burrell
rather than cowardly bell-bottom-
wearing Scooby-Doo-owning
slacker Shaggy.)

k) Brings toy in mouth to human.
Begs human to throw toy. Human
tries to take toy from canine's
mouth. Canine gets annoyed and
refuses to let go. Human gives up.
Canine begs human to throw toy...

l) Sees tail. Surprised by tail. Wants
to catch tail to examine it more
closely. Reaches for tail. Tail stays
out of reach. Reaches faster for
tail. Tail still stays out of reach.
Begins to spin faster and faster
while chasing tail. Spins fast
enough to drill a hole into earth's
crust and all the way out the other
side to Australia. Continues to
chase tail in Australia but even
more confused now as spinning
in different direction.

m) Loathes hoovers. Regards them
either as scary roaring monster
which can always find dog
wherever it hides or as erratically
moving animal to be herded by
barking, chasing and nipping.
Either way, regards hoover's
eventual silencing and return
to understairs kennel as famous
victory. Rover Rovers 1 Vacuum
United 0.

n) Nail-clipping day. This is World War
Three. Message to human: when
you bring your nail-clippers you'd
better bring your 'A'-game too.

o) Regards Squirrel Hell and Dog Heaven as the same place.

p) Of pale dogs such as Golden Retriever, to (a) roll on freshly mown grass until resembles the Incredible Hulk Dog (b) go into muddy areas until resembles a pint of Guinness.

q) Of large dogs, to perform complex calculus instantaneously on a Sunday morning in order to work out where in the kitchen to lie, and in what configuration, in order to cause maximum inconvenience to those preparing Sunday lunch.

s) Loves going in car when trip involves walks at the other end.

t) Hates going in car when trip involves vets at the other end.

u) Can somehow tell the difference even when human acting all cool and 'no biggie' and definitely NOT mentioning the word 'vet' at any time HOW DOES THE DOG KNOW? And if dog knows that then why can't dog pick six numbers on a Saturday night?

s) Loves nothing more than (a) locating malodorous substance (b) rolling in it. Cowpats good. Fox poo better. Can't understand why human gets so upset. I mean, have you smelt the aftershave he's wearing? Have you? And he calls me stinky boy?

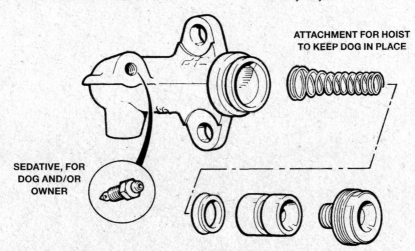

ATTACHMENT FOR HOIST
TO KEEP DOG IN PLACE

SEDATIVE, FOR
DOG AND/OR
OWNER

FIG 6•12 **CANINE BEHAVIOUR MODULE: THE CLIPPING OF THE NAILS**

Owner feedback

Owners like to give their dogs all kinds of different names. This is pointless. Every dog in the world knows it's called the same name: Hoozagoodboy. And every dog in the world knows that it must answer the same 10-question quiz on a daily basis.

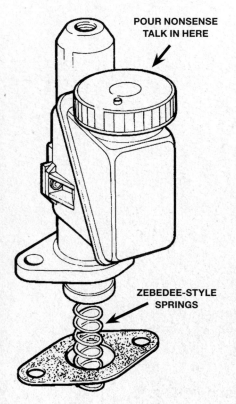

POUR NONSENSE TALK IN HERE

ZEBEDEE-STYLE SPRINGS

FIG 6•13 **CANINE ENERGY: THE SOURCE**

Asinine human questions

1 Who's a good boy?
2 Who is it?
3 WHO'S A GOOD BOY?
4 Is it you?
5 Is it?
6 Are you a good boy?
7 Are you my best boy?
8 Are you?
9 Are you really?
10 You're my good boy, aren't you?

Correct canine answers

1 I am.
2 I told you. I am.
3 I heard you the first time.
4 (sighing) Yes.
5 Still yes.
6 For the love of God.
7 I am losing the will to live.
8 How do you hold down a job?
9 I really think you might be mildly cretinous.
10 I'll be anything you like if you just shut up.

What we say: Got Snoop Dogg on the iPod and gonna walk to the car park. **What they hear:** gfegf dog hfjehwrgfjwrh walk jfhtjhrgj park.

Small vs big dogs

Canine models come in all shapes and sizes. Should you go for a small city-sized model or a big old SUV? Too small and you're basically owning a glorified rat: too big and you've got yourself a little horse. This table will help you work your way through the minefield of considerations.

Consideration	Small dog	Big dog
Travelling	Easy to transport in car. Welcome in most restaurants.	Getting them into car can be like scrum training with the All Blacks. Most restaurants will give you the 'are you taking the piss?' look if you try and bring them in.
Behaviour	Excitable and yappy. Always looking for a fight. If you cross a punchy dog with a psycho cat you'd get Begbie from *Trainspotting*.	Know they can lay the smackdown if need be, so much more chilled. Speak softly and carry a big stick. Which the owner can then throw.
Expense	Less.	More.
Mess	Less.	More.
Food	Find human food harder to reach unless can work out chair/table/chest of drawers assault course. A small amount of wrong food can be dangerous.	Can get human food much more easily. A small amount of wrong food can be harmless.
Urban living	Fits inside small apartments better. Can hide from landlord more easily if need be.	May be too big for urban apartments.

Central Processing Unit

Even the stupidest dog is actually pretty intelligent, as it has persuaded a human to water, feed, love and shelter it. Somewhere along the path of evolution, a wolf thought to himself 'all this roaming around and howling at the moon is all well and good, but it's also quite tiring always being on the lookout for food and predators, and Jeff's got a nice place over there, so let's go and see if we can cadge some stuff off the humans. OK, guys, try and look cute so the humans take pity on us. Imagine we're on a Hallmark card. What's Hallmark? Never mind, I'll explain later.'

Nature may be red in tooth and claw, but the wolves which suppressed this most successfully ended up living longer. For dogs, humanity is one giant welfare state.

The five most intelligent dogs are the Border Collie, Poodle, German Shepherd Dog, Golden Retriever and Doberman Pinscher.

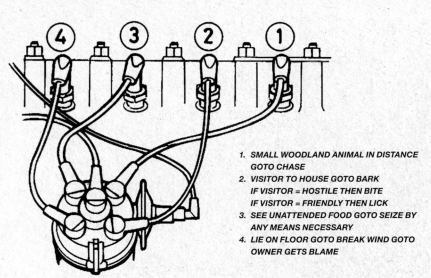

1. SMALL WOODLAND ANIMAL IN DISTANCE GOTO CHASE
2. VISITOR TO HOUSE GOTO BARK
   IF VISITOR = HOSTILE THEN BITE
   IF VISITOR = FRIENDLY THEN LICK
3. SEE UNATTENDED FOOD GOTO SEIZE BY ANY MEANS NECESSARY
4. LIE ON FLOOR GOTO BREAK WIND GOTO OWNER GETS BLAME

FIG 6•14 **SYNAPTIC LINKS: STIMULI AND REACTIONS IN THE DOG BRAIN**

⚠ Canine intelligence: Main facets

The average dog can learn 165 words, and some can learn 250 words. How many of these words are printable in a family publication like HAYNES EXPLAINS is another matter entirely. Dogs can also count up to four or five. They use the calculator on their iPhones for six and above.

1. Instinctive intelligence

What a dog was bred for, basically. Herding dogs were bred to herd animals. Guard dogs were bred to guard things, retrievers to retrieve, pointers to point (not to be confused with the Pointer Sisters and their exhortation to Jump! For My Love) and greyhounds to run around like headless chickens for 17 minutes a day and sleep for the other 23 hours 43 minutes.

2. Adaptive intelligence

What a dog can learn to do for himself. Using his experience to avoid making the same mistakes over and over again (though there's always one who's totally clueless. Or in my case two, as I have two greyhounds who always chase birds, deer and rabbit and have never caught any of them and wouldn't know what to do if they did).

3. Obedience intelligence

Responding to a master's command. Especially important for guide dogs, police dogs, search-and-rescue dogs, assistance dogs etc. Obviously not shared by Fenton – full name 'Fenton Fenton Fenton Fenton FENTON Fenton Oh-Jesus-Christ Oh-Jesus-Christ FENTONNNN Oh-Christ' – of YouTube/ Richmond Park/deer fame.

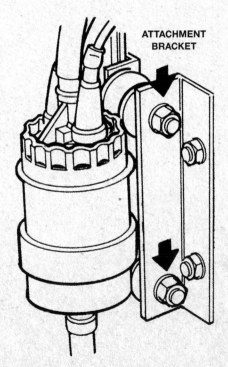

ATTACHMENT BRACKET

FIG 6•15 **CANINE IQ MEASURING APPLIANCE**

Famous models

Lassie
Everyone's favourite collie. Got a lot of people out of a lot of scrapes. Films included *Lassie Come Home*, *Courage of Lassie* and *Lassie's Great Adventure*. Films did not include Lassie Can't Be Arsed Today, Lassie In Heat and Lassie Has Fired Her Agent And Wants To Renegotiate Her Contract.

Hound of the Baskervilles
A bloodhound/mastiff cross which didn't bark in the night, which was how Sherlock Holmes knew it was him, or something like that. Obviously not the little yapping so-and-so at number 46 which must have vocal cords of titanium to keep up that incessant noise.

Toto
Terrier who accompanies Dorothy to Oz, never talks even when all the other animals around him are prattling away and somehow forbears from replying 'well, duh' when Dorothy informs him they're not in Kansas any more.

Snowy
Talking wire fox terrier and faithful sidekick to intrepid reporter Tintin. Often shows more sense than all the humans put together. Brave even against much bigger animals, but suffers from arachnophobia (though not anoraknophobia, if some of Tintin's more questionable fashion choices are anything to go by).

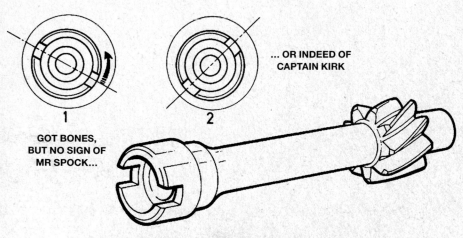

1

2

... OR INDEED OF
CAPTAIN KIRK

GOT BONES,
BUT NO SIGN OF
MR SPOCK...

FIG 6•16 **EVERY DOG'S ULTIMATE DREAM: THE REGENERATING BONE**

⚠ Canine dictionary

Word	Definition
Doge	Head of medieval Venice. Nothing to do with dogs at all.
Dogfight	Like a catfight, but between fighter jets and without people shrieking 'go on, scratch her face!'
Dogfish	A fish who is happy he's not a catfish but pretty pissed off about everything else.
Dogger	A canine's favourite place in the Shipping Forecast.
Doggerel	Female dogs from the West Country.
Doggone	Missing canine. Associated with dogcomebackwhenhungry.
Doghouse	Where the man of the house goes when he's in disfavour. The dog is always in the manhouse so thinks this is very funny.
Dogleg	Associated with the kind of gearbox that dogmatics don't like.
Dogmatic	A car for dogs who don't like manual gearboxes.
Dogsbody	Lowly worker dog.

Snoopy
Beagle in real life, World War I flying ace in his dreams. Lives in a kennel which is larger inside than outside and doubles as the Sopwith Camel in his imaginary alternate life. Constantly rejected as a writer. Don't worry, mate, we've all been there.

Reservoir Dogs
Dressed all in black and white. A bit like *101 Dalmatians* but with guns. No reservoirs, though.

Dogging
'I'm just taking the dog out for a walk, love.' 'OK. But don't be five hours this time and try not to get so muddy.'

Pavlov's Dog
Dog trained by Ivan Pavlov to associate the arrival of food with the ringing of a bell. If you ask a librarian for 'that book about Pavlov's Dog and Schrödinger's Cat', she'll say it rings a bell but she doesn't know whether it's on the shelf or not.

MODEL LINE: RODENT
Chassis types

Not all pets must be either feline or canine. There are several different types of rodents which make excellent pets. Depending on where you live and your level of commitment to pest control, you may already find yourself sharing house space with mice and rats. These do not count as pets.

HOLD BY LID AT TOP

FRONT

KEEP OTHER HAND WELL CLEAR OF HAMSTER

FIG 6•17 **PATENTED ANTI-BITE HANDY HAMSTER HANDLER**

Hamsters

Typically solitary animals which should be caged by themselves. All very easy for you to say, Mr Hamster, but there's a housing crisis, a bedroom tax and rents are skyrocketing, so you may have to bunk up with someone else. Hamsters which are used to being handled are usually friendly enough, but those which aren't used to it can bite. Hamsters love running on exercise wheels, and would point out to humans who laugh at this that they, hamsters, aren't the ones who drive ten miles each way to the gym just to run on a treadmill for half an hour.

Gerbils

Like hamsters, gerbils live two to three years on average. Their tail is furry and almost as long as their body. If you pick them up by that tail they will be extremely unhappy and let you know in no uncertain terms. Unlike grumpy chops Greta Garbo I-want-to-be-alone hamsters, gerbils are very social and like nothing more than a good chinwag/party/orgy. They're less prone to biting than hamsters, but are so energetic that they can be hard to keep hold of.

Mice

Very small, very fast, like to play and can be great fun to watch. Not so keen on cats, for obvious reasons, though all mice worship the god Jerry and avidly watch his repeated escapes from and escapades with the hapless Tom. Males tend to fight if left alone with other males – so what's new?

Rats

We've had a call from a Mr UB40 saying there's a rat in his kitchen what is he going to do? Anyone with any suggestions, please phone in. Rats are very social and are good pets despite the bad rep they get from some quarters. They are intelligent, curious and active, and when they're content they grind their teeth. Apparently. They can be taught basic tricks, though probably not anything as advanced as sawing a woman in half or the card-in-the-orange one. Before we go, we've heard back from Mr UB40, who tells us he's gonna get that rat that's what he's going to do he's gonna get that rat. And also, Roland Rat was not a real rat and should not be confused with:

a) Roland from Grange Hill
b) Roland synthesizers
c) Roland Orzabal of Tears For Fears
d) Childe Rowland
e) Roland Garros

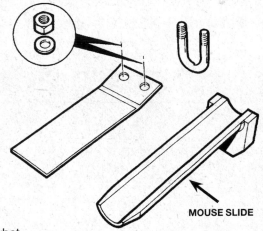

MOUSE SLIDE

FIG 6•18 **BECAUSE RODENTS NEED PLAYGROUNDS TOO**

Guinea Pigs

They have gentle temperaments in general, though they're rather annoyed that their name always gets used as a synonym for 'test experiment subjects' and wish they had at least put a decent IP lawyer onto the case when it all started to keep the royalties coming in. Are secretly envious but try not to gossip about the Skinny Guinea Pig who gets all the modelling gigs.

Rabbits

Not rodents, but they're nearer rodents than they are any of the next three categories. Traditionally popular pets. Pros: introduce your children to sex education early. Cons: *Fatal Attraction*.

MODEL LINE: GOLDFISH
Topping up fluids

Goldfish are widely considered to be unintelligent and have poor memory. This means that – sorry, what was I saying? Oh yes. Scientists now think goldfish are smarter than previously thought, though given that the 'previously thought' baseline was a notch or two up from a single-cell amoeba, this may be less impressive than it sounds at first.

Goldfish jokes

a) Two goldfish are in a tank. One turns to the other and says 'do you know how to drive this thing?'

b) What did the goldfish say when he swam into a wall? 'Dam.'

d) What do you call a goldfish with no eyes? Goldfsh.

A man walks into a cafe with a goldfish under his arm. He asks the owner 'Do you sell fish cakes?' 'No', says the owner. 'That's a shame,' says the man. 'It's his birthday today.'

FLAKE FOOD
(BASIC NUTRITION)
IN HERE

FROZEN FOOD
(BRINE SHRIMP, WORMS) IN HERE

HOUSEHOLD FOOD
(SHREDDED GREENS)
IN HERE

FIG 6•19 **GIANT GOLDFISH GASTRONOMIC GADGET**

⚠ Social Goldfish

Goldfish are a social species and enjoy being together. No, not because they're so stupid that they have to reintroduce themselves to each other every five minutes. (Most goldfish will recognise the person who feeds them most regularly and will swim excitedly towards the edge of the tank when they see them, but they will hide when strangers come along.) Solitary fish are prone to depression and lethargy. The Swiss have outlawed keeping goldfish on their own as it contravenes animal-welfare legislation there.

This is all well and good, but:

i) This is a nation in which it's illegal to flush the toilet at night in certain urban areas.

ii) This is a nation which frowns on people wearing swimming costumes in saunas as nudity is more healthy.

iii) How do they enforce the no single goldfish rule? Are there special detachments of Goldfish Police who mount dawn raids on suspected offenders? If so, does a Goldfish Policeman admit what he does to his friends and family?

You may think the Swiss are strange, but there are plenty of good things about the country – not least the flag, which is a big plus.

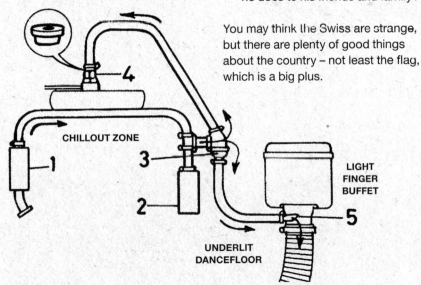

FIG 6•20 **AIN'T NO PARTY LIKE A GOLDFISH PARTY**

MODEL LINE: REPTILE
Exotic imports

Reptiles are in general cool pets: a little different, a little wackier than the norm. They also make good pets in general. They're lower maintenance than cats and dogs: they need feeding less often, they need grooming less often, they are less needy for attention, they don't need walking, they're quiet, and so on. The kind of reptiles usually kept as pets are far less likely to cause injury than a dog's bite or a cat's claws. And reptiles' mild (or not-so-mild) exoticness means they may foster more interest in the natural world amongst children who keep them as pets. Nature documentaries concentrate far more on reptiles than on hamsters. Sorry, hamsters.

Good reptile starter pets include the crested and leopard geckoes, the bearded dragon, the blue tongue skink, the corn snake and the ball python. Bad reptile starter pets include anacondas and reticulated pythons. Don't let a reticulated python sleep at the bottom of your bed – not because it might measure you up to eat you (that's an urban legend) but because it will make your friends think you're weird. And they will have a point.

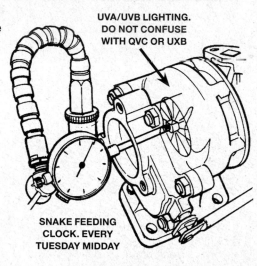

UVA/UVB LIGHTING. DO NOT CONFUSE WITH QVC OR UXB

SNAKE FEEDING CLOCK. EVERY TUESDAY MIDDAY

FIG 6•21 **REPTILE CAGE: MAINTAINING THE OPTIMUM ENVIRONMENT**

It is a little-known fact that Boy George kept a reptile as a pet. It was a rather hyperactive animal to start with, but Boy George would sing songs to it and gradually it became a calmer chameleon.

⚠ Should you get a snake?

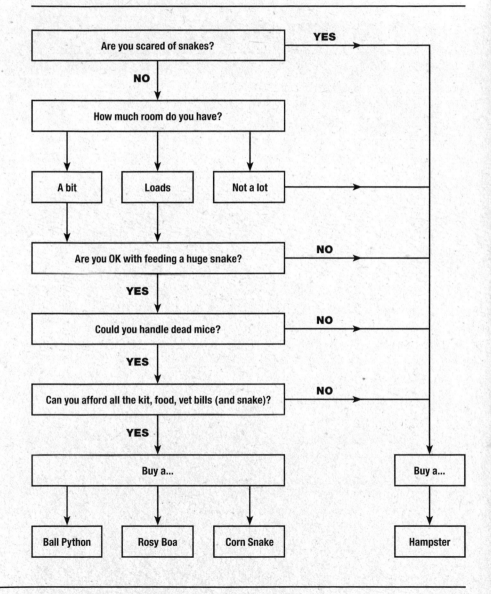

Are you scared of snakes? — **YES** →

NO ↓

How much room do you have?

- A bit
- Loads
- Not a lot →

Are you OK with feeding a huge snake? — **NO** →

YES ↓

Could you handle dead mice? — **NO** →

YES ↓

Can you afford all the kit, food, vet bills (and snake)? — **NO** →

YES ↓

Buy a...

- Ball Python
- Rosy Boa
- Corn Snake

Buy a...

- Hampster

MODEL LINE: AVIAN
Air conditioning

Birds are also popular pets. Well, some birds, obviously. Not ones like albatrosses or vultures.

Budgies

Small, playful and affectionate. Much quieter than some bigger birds. Enjoy looking at themselves in mirrors and love to show off when they play. Often smuggled by men wearing swimming trunks a size or two too small.

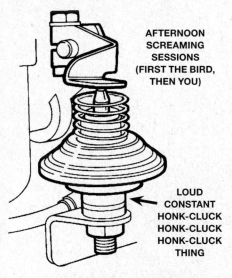

AFTERNOON SCREAMING SESSIONS (FIRST THE BIRD, THEN YOU)

LOUD CONSTANT HONK-CLUCK HONK-CLUCK HONK-CLUCK THING

FIG 8•23 **THE EARWORM EQUIPMENT: DRIVING REPETITIVE BIRD SOUNDS DEEP INTO YOUR SKULL**

Parrots

Good talkers and mimics. Amusing in general. Less so when your frenemy comes round and your parrot tells her EXACTLY what you've been saying about her. Good size: not too large and not too small.

Canaries

Very vocal and vibrantly coloured. Female canaries don't sing: only male canaries do. Bet Simon Cowell wished he'd known that before trying to put together Canaries Aloud. Especially popular in the Norwich area (canaries, not Cowell). Now wise to the old 'let's go down the mine' trick. Come to think of it, probably fairly relieved at the decline in the mining industry full stop. Don't much like being handled.

DO: teach your bird to say 'hello'
DO: teach your bird to say its name
DO: teach your bird a few lines from a favourite song

DON'T: teach your bird to say 'f*** off'
DON'T: teach your bird to use offensive nicknames
DON'T: teach your bird if your favourite song is rap

⚠ Keeping a bird

Pros	Cons
Intelligent. Learns things fast.	May learn the wrong things fast. Liable to swear like a docker when your mother-in-law's round.
Easy to care for: can be kept in a cage and doesn't need walking/housetraining	Shouldn't be kept in a cage the whole time.
Easy to train.	Need mental stimulation or can develop emotional problems. Won't lie on couch long enough for proper psychiatric diagnosis.
Keep themselves reasonably clean and like to preen themselves.	Like to preen their owners too. Often with less gentleness than their owners would like.
Relatively inexpensive to keep.	Should have regular vets' checks.
Live a long time.	May outlive you.

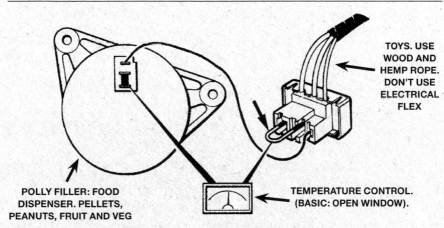

TOYS. USE WOOD AND HEMP ROPE. DON'T USE ELECTRICAL FLEX

POLLY FILLER: FOOD DISPENSER. PELLETS, PEANUTS, FRUIT AND VEG

TEMPERATURE CONTROL. (BASIC: OPEN WINDOW).

FIG 8·24 **PARROT HABITAT: SETTING UP ITS CAGE JUST RIGHT**

Fault diagnosis

Fault	Diagnosis	Treatment
Cat wants to go out.	It's a cat and it operates by cat logic.	Let the cat out.
Cat wants to come in.	It's a cat and it operates by cat logic.	Let the cat in.
Cat wants to go out again.	It's a cat and it operates by cat logic.	Let the cat out again.
Cat wants to come in again.	It's a cat and it operates by cat logic.	Let the cat in again.
Cat wants to go out again.	It's a cat and it operates by cat logic.	Let the cat out again.
Cat wants to come in again.	It's a cat and it operates by cat logic.	Let the cat in again.
Cat wants to go out again.	It's a cat and it operates by cat logic.	Let the cat out again.
Cat wants to come in again.	It's a cat and it operates by cat logic.	Let the cat in again.
Cat wants to go out again.	It's a cat and it operates by cat logic.	Let the cat out again.
Cat wants to come in again.	It's a cat and it operates by cat logic.	Let the cat in again.
Cat wants to go out again.	It's a cat and it operates by cat logic.	Let the cat out again.
Cat wants to come in again.	It's a cat and it operates by cat logic.	Let the cat in again.
Cat wants to go out again.	It's a cat and it operates by cat logic.	Let the cat out again.
Cat wants to come in again.	It's a cat and it operates by cat logic.	Let the cat in again.
Cat wants to go out again.	It's a cat and it operates by cat logic.	Let the cat out again.
Cat wants to come in again.	It's a cat and it operates by cat logic.	Let the cat in again.
Cat wants to go out again.	It's a cat and it operates by cat logic.	Let the cat out again.
Cat wants to come in again.	It's a cat and it operates by cat logic.	Let the cat in again.
Cat wants to go out again.	It's a cat and it operates by cat logic.	Let the cat out again.
Cat wants to come in again.	It's a cat and it operates by cat logic.	Let the cat in again.

Conclusion

Getting and keeping pets is not for everyone. Pets require time and money, and many people do not have enough of either. Young children may like the idea of a pet but baulk at the actual responsibility which comes with owning one, and with very young children there is always the safety issue of the damage a pet can do to them if left alone even for a moment. Some people are allergic to one animal or another. If you live in a city and keep a dog, two things are for sure: they will poop on the street and you will be required to clean it up.

Pets don't tend to keep to a human schedule: I've lost count of the number of times I've gone downstairs bleary eyed at three in the morning because the dogs are barking at some hapless small woodland animal/at each other/for the hell of it, and asking them 'how would you feel if I woke you up for no reason?' doesn't tend to get an especially helpful reaction (or indeed any reaction at all other than their usual state of excitable idiocy).

But the upsides are also sizeable. A pet gives you love which is pretty much unconditional, and in doing so can comfort you when you're down and relax you when you're stressed. It's not for nothing that dogs in particular are trained to provide assistance to those unable to fully fend for themselves. Medium-sized and large dogs can also provide a level of home and personal security. The need to walk dogs can get you out of the house and provide exercise (and also social contact: with the possible exception of babies, nothing breaks the conversational ice like a dog, though that broken ice can turn frosty again very quickly if your dog goes for their dog...).

And if you take an animal from a shelter, you are not only making room at that shelter but just as importantly giving an abandoned or abused animal a second chance at a much better, more loving life. We have two rescue greyhounds, one of which was very badly beaten in her racing days. We can't erase or undo that, but we can at least make the second half of her life better than the first half was – and she in turn makes our lives better too.

Titles in the Haynes Explains series

001	*Babies*	ISBN 978 1 78521 102 7
002	*Teenagers*	ISBN 978 1 78521 103 4
003	*Marriage*	ISBN 978 1 78521 104 1
004	*Pensioners*	ISBN 978 1 78521 105 8
005	*Christmas*	ISBN 978 1 78521 152 2
006	*Pets*	ISBN 978 1 78521 153 9
007	*The French*	ISBN 978 1 78521 154 6
008	*Germans*	ISBN 978 1 78521 155 3
009	*The British*	ISBN 978 1 78521 150 8
010	*Americans*	ISBN 978 1 78521 151 5
011	*The Home*	ISBN 978 1 78521 157 7
012	*Football*	ISBN 978 1 78521 156 0

Now that Haynes has explained Pets, you can progress to our full size manuals on car maintenance (save money for those vet bills), *Aquarium Manual* (in-depth goldfish maintenance), *Chicken Manual* (pets with benefits), *Meat Manual* (let's not go there).

There are Haynes manuals on just about everything – but let us know if we've missed one.

Haynes.com